Feast of the Pansexualists

Jon Lange

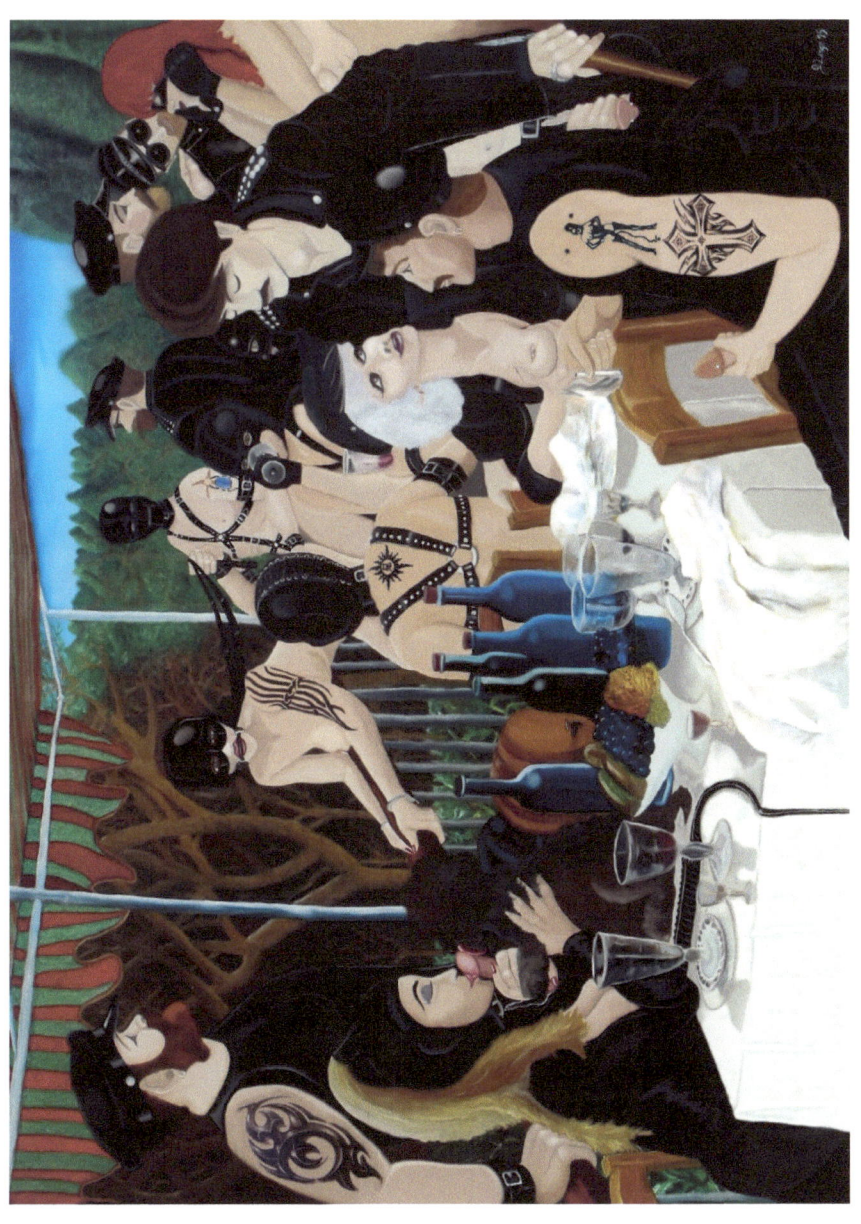

Other works by the same author:
Memories/Remorse
Knobby the Knobhead
The Big O Show
At the Heart of Ignorance

Contents

'A feast for the Supreme Ritual, and a feast for the Equinox of the Gods.
A feast for fire and a feast for water; a feast for life and a greater feast for death!
A feast every day in your hearts in the joy of my rapture!
A feast every night unto Nu, and the pleasure of uttermost delight!'

(Book of the Law, II. 40-43)

PREFACE

The following essay was written in the summer of 1995 to accompany an exhibit of my painting 'Feast of the Pansexualists.' The latter was put on display in the local nightclub dedicated to a night of fetishism. There were plenty of other things to feast your eyes on that night; latex, leather and bondage gear, people playing sub-dom roles, high-heeled Mistresses cracking their whips, transvestites dressed in their best frocks, and slave-girls wearing nothing at all except perhaps the odd leather belt. It was an interesting night.

To help people appreciate my painting, I gave out this essay in the form of a small booklet so at least they could form a better idea what it was all about, and explained that it was based on the famous painting by Renoir, with a very small photo of both paintings side by side at the back of the booklet. Some of the patrons that night recognised the source for my inspiration; some did not. As it was only a small edition and was given out for free, it is understandable that I ran out of copies of the booklet before the night was through. Those who were fortunate enough to get a copy hopefully found my essay to be enlightening. Many people made positive comments about the painting and encouraged me to further my pursuits in this field.

As my painting was based on Renoir's work exactly, which measured 65 x 48 inches, it was rather large, and its size no doubt made it stand out in the dark, dingy corner of the club where it was propped up against the wall above all the velvet cushioned seats. It could not help but be noticed. I remember there was a stall positioned next to me with a young lady offering hand-painted henna designs for £10. When she got a customer they would be seated facing towards the painting whilst they were having a particular part of their anatomy painted, and most of her customers couldn't take their eyes off it.

Some even wanted to buy it, offering me large sums of money, to which I politely refused. Nowadays, of course, it would be possible to get a digital photo of the painting and post it online so that everyone could download it for free. But we are talking about the pre-internet days when such things were not possible for most people; so they had to make do with a rather poorly produced booklet.

The painting was just a bit of fun. It was an idea I came up with when I was undergoing a great deal of pain (as explained in the essay). I needed something to take my mind of the agony I was in, and this image popped into my head and I quickly sketched it out when I got home. I did some research on Renoir's 'Luncheon of the Boating Party' and took note of the actual measurements of the original, went out and bought a large board (I couldn't afford a canvas of that size) and coated it with a white acrylic base coat for the oils to adhere to, smoothed it down to a fine finish, wiped it down with a wet cloth and left it to dry. I next took a photo of Renoir's painting from a print in an art book and, using a projector, projected the slide onto the board and sketched very roughly the actual position of the people and the objects as they appeared. My rule was to keep any changes to the absolute minimum. If a figure had to be moved it was only by a few inches, with perhaps the torso bent slightly forward so that it was possible to see what was really going on behind that person.

I tried to stick as closely as possible to the original as I wanted it to be recognized straightaway. I wanted people to see what my painting was based on. However, I had never used oils before. I found them to be messy and took forever to dry before you could apply the brush to an adjacent area without accidentally leaning the side of your hand on the wet paint. In the end, I resorted to using a stick to lean against, which was something I could never get to grips with. Realising that I was no adept when it came to painting with this medium, I went off and did a few practice small pieces of an unrelated nature, and learnt how to mix the paint and blend in the colours that I wanted. My medium had always been either water colours or gouache, so to attempt to replicate a masterpiece like Renoir's work was probably I bit too ambitious on my part. And I found his style to be almost impossible to copy.

I had never liked Impressionism; to me it was always vague and indefinable. The artists are trying to give an impression of what they feel about the scene being painted. Often in their landscape paintings there is no definite border between land and sky; they tend to blend into each other so that there is no visible demarcation of the two. This is something I found almost impossible to duplicate with Renoir's 'Luncheon' as you could not tell sometimes where the shrubbery in the background stopped and the sky started, rather like a badly out of focus photo. All my attempts to duplicate his method failed. Should I have been an artist by trade, a forger of the masters, or an advocate of this school of art perhaps, then my job would have been a hell of a lot easier. As it was, in the end I had to admit defeat; I was no master, and nowhere near to capturing Renoir at his best, if not his worst.

So I abandoned the idea of doing an Impressionist-style painting and reverted back to my own style, mixing the oils with plenty of linseed to help dilute them so that the paint would dry quicker and I could get on and complete the picture in time for the fetish party. I only had two weeks left before the great event was due to start, so I hastily finished off the painting, and rather regretted doing that as it appeared to be rushed in its execution. I don't know how long Renoir took to paint his picture, but I can imagine it must have been over several weeks in 1881. Also, he had been painting for a number of years; I had only just taken up the habit two years previously, so I was still learning.

My success, in the end, is questionable. I don't believe it to be a brilliant picture. In fact, I would say I failed to a certain extent. It certainly did not match my expectations, and my impatience towards the end ruined an otherwise reasonable effort. If I had the chance again I would probably spend longer on the actual painting of the piece itself, applying brush to board more diligently. But as it stands, it is not bad, and the many people who have seen it over the years have made positive comments, especially when put against a reproduction of Renoir's work. They could see the similarity and what I was trying to do, knowing that I had always been interested in fetishism and the so-called 'modern primitive' culture for a long time. One acquaintance liked it so much that the next time he came round with his girlfriend the first thing he did was to drag her into my kitchen where it is permanently on display so she could have a good look at it as well. Another could be heard chuckling to himself in the kitchen when he was surveying it, so presumably he not only liked it but also found it amusing. But none, out of all the people who have seen it, have found it to be offensive in any way; nor did they find it obscene. It helped that they were all open-minded and not prudish at all. Nor did any comment that it was pornographic, despite the private parts on display and the context of the picture itself. As it is a work of art I doubt very much whether it could be called pornographic. Great artists have always painted the human figure in the nude, both male and female. In my case I have simply taken Renoir's work one step further.

I'm not an artist; I only pretend to be one. If anything, I am a dilettante. I like playing at being an artist when the mood suits me. But I have to be very strongly inspired for me to do anything the least bit creative, especially when it comes to putting brush to canvas. As far as I am concerned, however, it is the meaning behind the painting that is important rather than the execution thereof.

'Feast of the Pansexualists' was, in the end, meant to sum up my philosophy. In the following essay I hope I have succeeded better as an essayist than an artist.

Jon Lange
Summer 2014

'FEAST OF THE PANSEXUALISTS'

AN ALTERNATIVE VERSION OF RENOIR'S
'LUNCHEON OF THE BOATING PARTY'
(Revised 2014[1])

'There is nothing but sexuality. This is the only certainty. All attempts to categorise or limit sexuality's inherent qualities are the result of man's failure at coming to terms with this powerful force. Out of his arrogance he foolishly believes he is its master, whereas in actuality he is its slave. The dictates of sexuality can never be ignored. He tries to channel it into socially conforming ways, imposing limits on it, seeking to stem its tides, to curb its flow and ends up being neurotic and wonders why. Any restrictions on sexuality are not only unnatural; they are also inimical and detrimental to the well being of the individual.

He must learn this lesson now: There is no homo, bi, hetro. These are labels, illusory. There is only sexuality, and he who is free of restriction is able to manifest his sexuality as he wills, for the Pansexualist knows he is all-sexuality, and through his openness he becomes All; Pan!'

(The Pansexualist, in
Black Leather Bible[2])

Out of all the works of the so-called great masters of art there has been one piece of work I have always been compelled to loathe; Renoir's 'Luncheon of the Boating Party,'[3] with its affected sense of *joi de vivre*, pretentious bonhomie, and the self-deluding view of life as something pleasant.

The trouble with Renoir, and other Impressionists for that matter, is their positivism; their need to define a category of life that is somehow full of joy and merriment, despite the existence of reality as harsh, cold and undiscriminating. In urban, industrial living, this attitude is absurd and redundant in a world that is corrupt and decadent. Renoir's work, and in particular this one under discussion, is a vain attempt to characterise the zeitgeist of his time. It miserably fails. It strives to set itself up as an affirmation of beauty, ennobling; where only a facade is visible, demonstrating how out of touch with reality he really was. I associate this with purchasers of art who have no taste and thus no morals or value judgements. Their judgement of what constitutes true art is based on a superficial approach to the subject that overrides all taste because it is non-existent.

It was therefore decided to render his opus in modern terms, stripped of all falsity and deceit. This was based on the following three principles:

1) To manifest the implicit sexuality inherent in the painting that he was too fearful to express himself due to moral and social constraints.
2) To undermine the petty bourgeois notion this painting exemplifies.
3) To take it to its fullest logical conclusion.

This would then abreact the absurdity of his work and raise it to a higher level of truth that he failed to achieve in his own lifetime.

The actual situation in which this particular piece of work was re-evolved in my mind is worth noting briefly.

During a trip to the dentist I was told a tooth was so bad that it would need to be extracted. It was on the lower jaw, right at the back, and had been causing me considerable discomfort for some time, so its removal was inevitable. However, the dentist did warn me that even under local anaesthetic the extraction would still be rather painful, and he was quite correct. Afterwards he advised me to sit in the waiting room and wait for the anaesthetic to wear off before even thinking of walking the short distance home. It was then, sitting alone in this white, nondescript, clean, disinfected room that I was forced to confront Renoir's work on the opposite wall, a painting I was never partial to ever since I had seen it as a child on my grand-mother's wall, one of those cheap prints in a cheap frame.

It was during this state of intense pain my eyes were averted to it and, in true Dalinian fashion, the painting underwent a transmogri-fication in my mind whereby the inherent sexual elements that suggested themselves, and were only visible subconsciously, came to the fore and in the process changed my pain to pleasure. In fact, I became so absorbed in this process of transformation that the pain was quite dissolved immediately. The result was a desire to catch the essence of the painting in its new format. The outcome is explained below.

'Feast of the Pansexualists' is a celebration of the divine diversity of the sexual manifold in man. It is an apotheosis of unconditioned desire freed from inhibition and an overt vignette of the beauty of truth; truth in this case rendered as the freedom from sin and the pernicious guilt-complex.

A conscious decision was made to keep the changes in the painting to an absolute minimum. The few re-arrangements that have been made were necessary to fulfil all the aforementioned principles. Gone are the modest blandishments that beset the original work; the smug, coy-look reminiscent of a faded past. Overt now is the con-temporary culture in which sexuality now finds itself. The overall impression is one of hegemony and openness, a satisfaction of sexual identity and response.

The day has given way to early evening. Yet this should not be taken as literal. With the oncoming of night the beautiful people have come out to play in all their fine regalia. Each piece of clothing is emblematic of their characters and symbolises the way they see themselves. This shifting to a new time zone has seen them evolve, each one moving into a sexual sphere that typifies their sexualities as a better way of expressing it.

The western mind has the in-built tendency to read from left to right, and so should this picture be read. The left side is the dark side of consciousness in man, as well as the subconscious, the domain of the dark forces that surface as instinct and desire, and the repository in man that is barely tapped due to repression and (in)correct social functioning. Macrocosmically, it is the western land, the land of the dead, the abode of the ever dying sun. It is represented in this painting as the dark woods, the realm of nature that is privy to fear, the abode of Pan[4] (the god of the libido); the unknown stalks us all in its intensity.

The right is the east, the side of light. It is portrayed accordingly with the light source being the opening in the canopy allowing the last vestiges of the setting sun to come through from the left. The left has always been associated with the dark mysterious realm. *Sinister*, in Latin, simply means *left,* suggestive of something forbidden. The right is the realm of life, the sun in its rising and hence abundant vegetation is shown, strong and vibrant. Thus the transition is one of coming out of the darkness, i.e. the closet-world of surreptitiousness, and into the light (of day)[5], the implication being that man should not be afraid of those inherent forces that move him which he attempts to hide from himself and others. The command is to not hide his vices behind virtuous words[6] but revel in his individual-ism in whatever form it may partake. There is no shame, there is no guilt in coming out, in facing reality. Each man and woman is a star[7], and as a star you should shine brightly, and be openly free to express your sexuality as you will with the assured knowledge that you are not acting contradictorily to your own true self and all that it comports.

The picture is saying on its most basic level that we must strip away all false idols, all false accretions that constitute false belief. These are seen to be but weaknesses, moral inhibitions that destroy man, not create him. This display of desire, as sovereignty, is the royal path that makes men not men but gods. This private little world is a microcosm that encapsulates the macrocosm as a supreme affirmation of desire in a global society where individuality is the norm not the exception, a society that is free from the sin of restriction[8]. This is borne out by the age range of the people portrayed; it features both young and old, whatever their orientation and persuasion. It is all-embracing. For sexuality, stripped free from its notions of what is right and what is acceptable, is in essence non-specific. Neither is anyone in charge; all here are equal, and respect each other accordingly. This is symbolised by the whip. In ancient Egypt the whip (or flail) was a symbol of power, and was always held in the right hand by the pharaoh, denoting he was in charge. To let go of the whip is to relinquish power. Here the whip lies idle on the table, in nobody's hands for no one is in charge.

Here all forms of sexuality are manifested. This is pansexuality *per se*, all-sexuality, for there is nothing but sexuality how ever it may manifest[9]. This transcends all previous categorisations of sexual behaviour like hetro/bi/homo which are seen in themselves to be equally illusory; they are merely labels. Sexuality is duality; once duality has been transcended sexuality becomes all, i.e. Pan. As already mentioned, Pan is the god of the woods. He represents nature uncorrupted by false belief. The heinous crime of restrictive thinking, i.e. the suppression of Pan, results in the atrophying of desire, the instinctive impulse towards objects that manifests as libido. Restriction brings with it the suffocation of instinct, the stifling of this impulse and consequently death of genius. Man does not become God, only a corpse.

Lastly, as regards actual content, there is nothing here that is meant to deliberately offend. A man free from sin will see only beauty here, not blasphemy, an affirmation of all that makes him a man; whereas the vulgar will see only vulgarity, their minds riddled with false belief. But of all the fleeting vicissitudes that beset us the one certainty is the omnipresence of sexuality and that a positive means of progression lies not in its repression (that will only result in neuroses, fear, guilt and loss of self), but in the adoption of the doctrines of pansexuality as the road to freedom and growth[10].

> And I rave; and I rape and I rip and I rend
> Everlasting, world without end,
> Mannikin, maiden, maenad, man,
> In the might of Pan.
> Io Pan! Io Pan Pan! Pan! Io Pan!
> (Crowley's *Hymn to Pan*[11])

NOTES TO THE 2014 EDITION

1. *Feast of the Pansexualists* was originally published privately in 1995 as a small booklet with a black and white plate in a limited edition of 50 copies. It consisted only of that plate and the essay. I have tidied the text of the essay and added notes to this edition to help clear up any misunderstandings.

2. *The Pansexualist* was a comment on my re-interpretation of the 15th card of the Major Arcana in the tarot deck, normally designated *The Devil*. I re-titled it *Pansexuality* in accordance with a transmission I received during magickal workings which would later be known as *Black Leather Bible*, a still unpublished text. The reason for its non-publication was due to its fragmentary form; when you are working with a current you tap into its source. Unfortunately, because of pressures at work (i.e. my 9 to 5 mundane job) I had to stop working with this current and lost contact with the source so only fragments remain. These will be published next year along with my new tarot designs and everything else relating to what I call the *Double Current*. The essay included here is an expansion of *The Pansexualist*.

3. Renoir's 'Luncheon of the Boating Party,' (1881). Pierre-Auguste Renoir (1841–1919) was a French artist who helped

to develop the Impressionist style and was renowned for his celebration of beauty and aesthetics. He was also devoted to feminine sensuality, as can be viewed in many of his paintings. This painting, *Le déjeuner des canotiers,* its French title, is well-known due to constant reprinting. Unfortunately, due to copyright restrictions, it cannot be reproduced here but a quick Google search will yield many photos of the painting. It was sold after his death in 1923 for $125,000 and is now housed in The Phillips Collection in Washington, D.C. It is probably his most famous painting.

It depicts his friends relaxing on a balcony at the Maison Fournaise along the river Seine in Chatou, France. The man seated on the right, the closest person to the viewer, is his artist friend Gustave Caillebotte. Renoir's future wife, Aline Charigot, is the woman playing with the dog on the left. The young woman with the straw hat leaning on the railings is the proprietor's daughter Louise-Alphonsine Fournaise. Her brother Alphonse Fournaise Junior is the large man who is also leaning on the railings. The man at the back with the top hat is Charles Ephrussi (a wealthy amateur art historian, collector, and editor of the *Gazette des Beaux-Arts*). The younger man he is talking to is probably Jules Laforgue, his personal secretary, but this is not certain. The woman drinking from a glass in the centre of the picture is the actress Ellen Andrée. Seated opposite her (with his back to us) is Baron Raoul Barbier. The three figures at the back and far right (the two men chatting up the woman) are Eugène Pierre Lestringez, Paul Lhote and the actress Jeanne Samary. The woman seated facing the man on the right in the foreground (Caillebotte) is the actress Angèle Legault. The man who is standing up and almost leaning over her is the journalist Adrien Maggiolo.

Note: According to the reference book I used in 1995 for the dimensions of Renoir's painting, it measured 65 by 48.

However, I note now on various websites its actual dimensions are 68 by 51. So there is a slight discrepancy by three inches, but at least my painting is in the correct proportion.

4. *Pan*, in Greek, literally means *All*. Therefore *Pansexuality* is *All-sexuality*.

5. In ancient Egypt the *Book of the Dead* (a set of spells buried with the mummy) was known as *Per-em-hru*. It has been translated as 'Coming forth by day,' 'Coming into the Light,' etc., meaning coming into full consciousness. Thus the ancient Egyptians believed that upon death the soul came into its own sphere where it received a new, second life.

6. *Not hide his vices behind virtuous words*. This is a reference to Crowley's the *Book of the Law*, a text hereinafter simply referred to as *AL*. The exact phrase is 'veil not your vices in virtuous words: these vices are my service.' (AL, II.52). This short book is the cornerstone of my philosophy. It was received by transmission through the scribe Aleister Crowley (1875-1947) in Cairo in 1904 and is, I believe, the pivotal moment in history that would later shift the whole western world into a new era with its sociological ramifications. If it wasn't for this small book there would be no openness about sexuality; no freedom of expression; no tolerance towards homosexuality; no enthusiasm to experiment with one's own identity, nor playing around with gender roles. As Crowley said himself in the introduction to this book, the changes it has brought about has seen an increase in what he called the 'epicene youth,' or ambiguous gender, where there is little distinction between men and women, all characterised by this book and its adumbration of the Aeon of the Child. And it even calls us children ('Come forth, o children, under the stars, & take your fill of love!' AL, I.12.) As children we play, and there has been no small sign of this playing when it comes to gender identity, as can be witnessed in the upsurge in fetish parties that have occurred over the last few decades with new clubs opening especially to cater for the child within, like the Torture Club, for example. This was all

brought about by this one little book. If it wasn't for the Law of Thelema (the Greek for *Will*), as embodied in this book, there would be no such thing as fetishism as we recognise it today. My painting embodies this idea and is a manifestation of what I call the *Double Current* (Thelema and S/M combined).

7.   'Every man and every woman is a star.' (AL, I.3)

8.   'The word of Sin is Restriction.' (AL, I.41)

9.   There is a cosmic law that states that anything that manifests on this plane automatically evokes its opposite. So therefore you cannot have light without darkness; heat without cold; dryness without wet; life without death; and man without woman. However, if we were to transcend this plane of duality all forms of opposites would cease to be; there would be no difference between any one thing and any other thing. This is represented by the epicene Biune one, a being of indiscriminate sex, one who is neither male nor female, but more than a hermaphrodite for it is capable of expressing itself in either way as male or female. The same goes for sexuality; sexuality is duality. Once you have transcended the plane of duality all opposites are obliterated and sexuality ceases to be; there is only a sense of being. However, when you come back down to this plane, the plane of duality, you are now free to manifest your sexuality in whatever way you will, because you know deep in your heart that things like homosexuality, bisexuality, heterosexuality, etc., are merely labels; they are meaningless because they have no meaning above the plane of duality. This is a hard concept for some people to grasp, but it has to be thoroughly introjected to be understood properly.

10.   It could be argued here that really 'pansexuality' is but another label and therefore no different from other labels like hetro, etc, which are equally illusory. This can be countered, however, by the fact that sexuality will always exist and therefore it will never escape the clutches of categorisation for we always compartmentalise our thinking,

especially towards others. For instance, when we meet somebody for the first time we automatically judge them, deciding whether we like them, dislike them, trust them, distrust them, etc. It is an innate habit that is almost impossible to quash. In the same way, we accept that different forms of sexuality exist. But rather than limit our thinking by using labels to compartmentalise, we should get into the habit of non-discrimination, non-judgement, and leave sexuality open so that it flows through us naturally like a current. Sexuality forms the seat of our identity, but in western society we are made to conform to one form of sexual behaviour rather than another. In the old days, homosexuality, for example, was treated like a disease as if there was something wrong with the person, or that he was in need of corrective therapy. Now, we accept that it exists and that for some it is a perfectly natural form of expression and sexual behaviour. But what we need to do is to override all this by knowing deeply that there is nothing but sexuality and that it should not be channelled into one form of behaviour or another, but left open. Only those who have transcended the plane of duality are really able to do this. Unfortunately, not everyone is capable of doing it. Therefore we need to change our thinking. We recognise that sexuality is diverse. Yet pansexuality embraces all forms of sexuality so it should be accepted as the norm regardless of whatever way it manifests.

11. The full text of Crowley's 'Hymn to Pan' can be found at the start of his *Magick in Theory and Practice* (or his *Magick*, edited by John Symonds and Kenneth Grant, pp. 125-7). Aleister Crowley, by the way, was an exemplary of pansexuality in that he was neither hetro nor homo nor bi. He was capable of expressing himself sexually in whatever way he chose to because he had transcended the plane of duality and his sexual behaviour reflected this. Freud would have called him 'polymorphously diverse.' I prefer to think he was a true Pansexualist. He is an example to us all.

APPENDIX

CLOSE-UP DETAIL

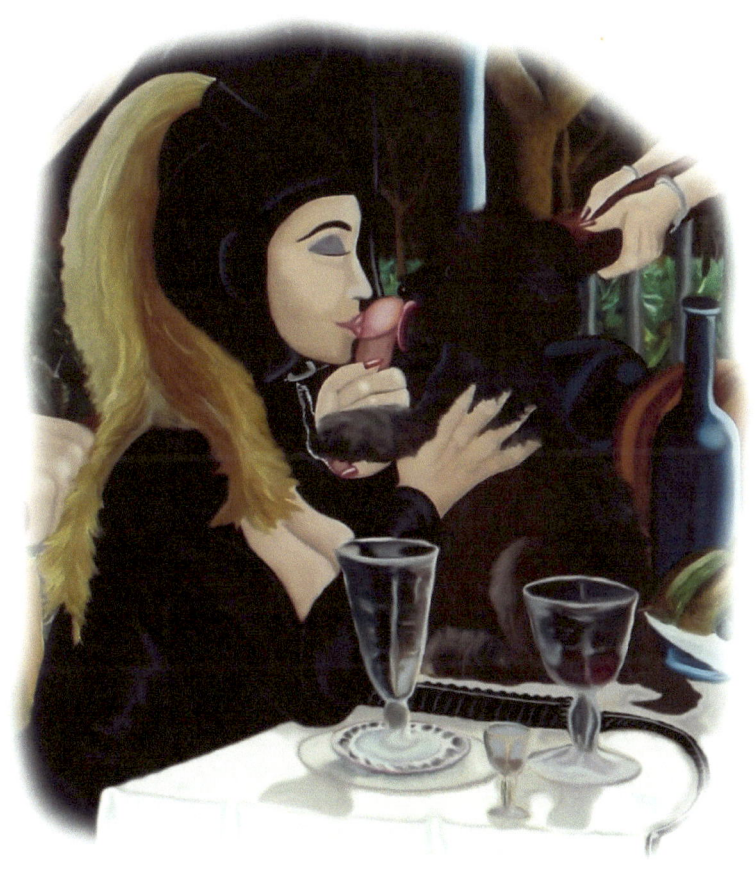

'Man's best friend?'

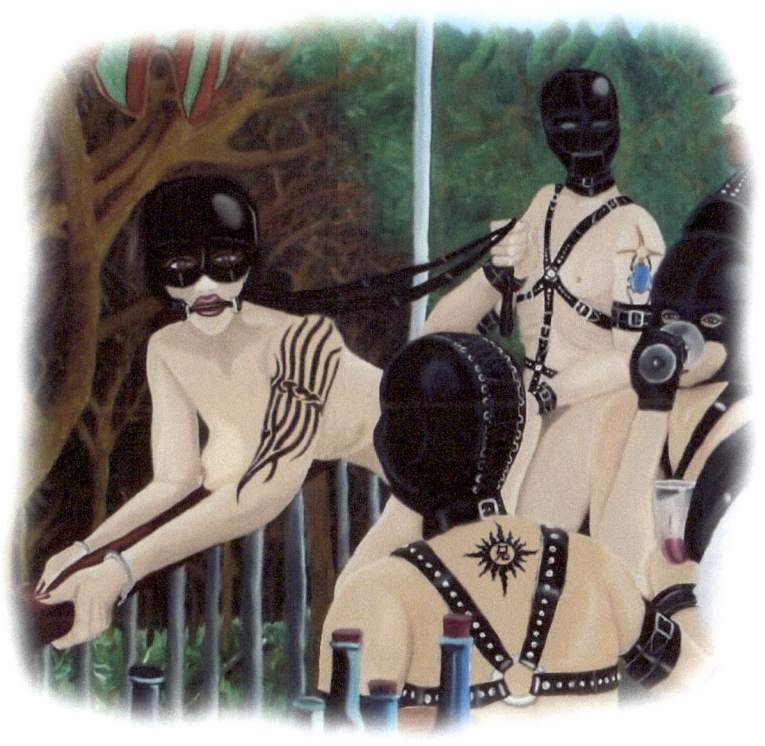

'Rear entry again, my dear?'

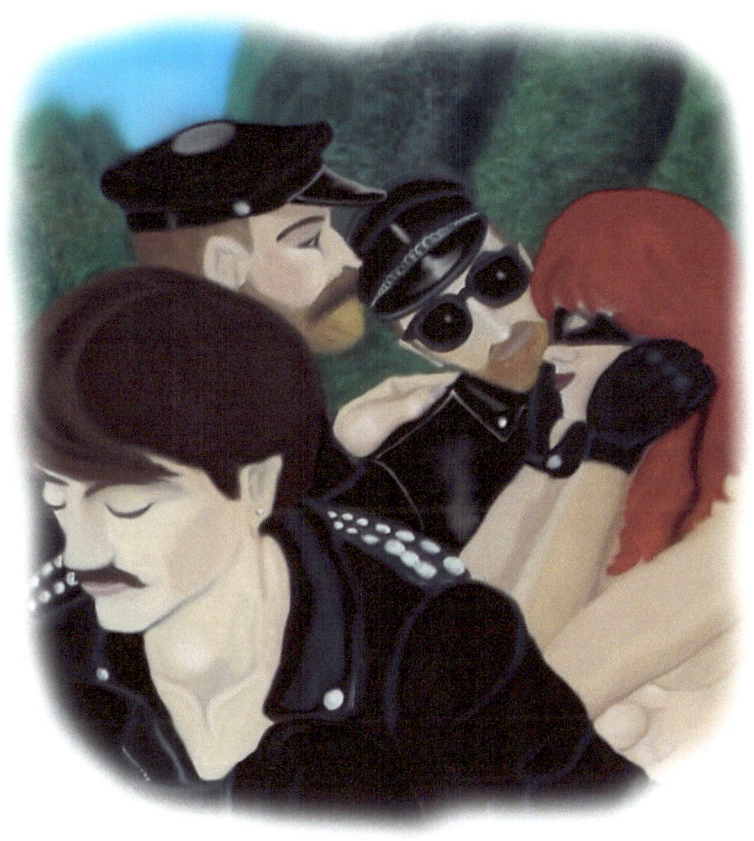

'Fancy a threesome?'

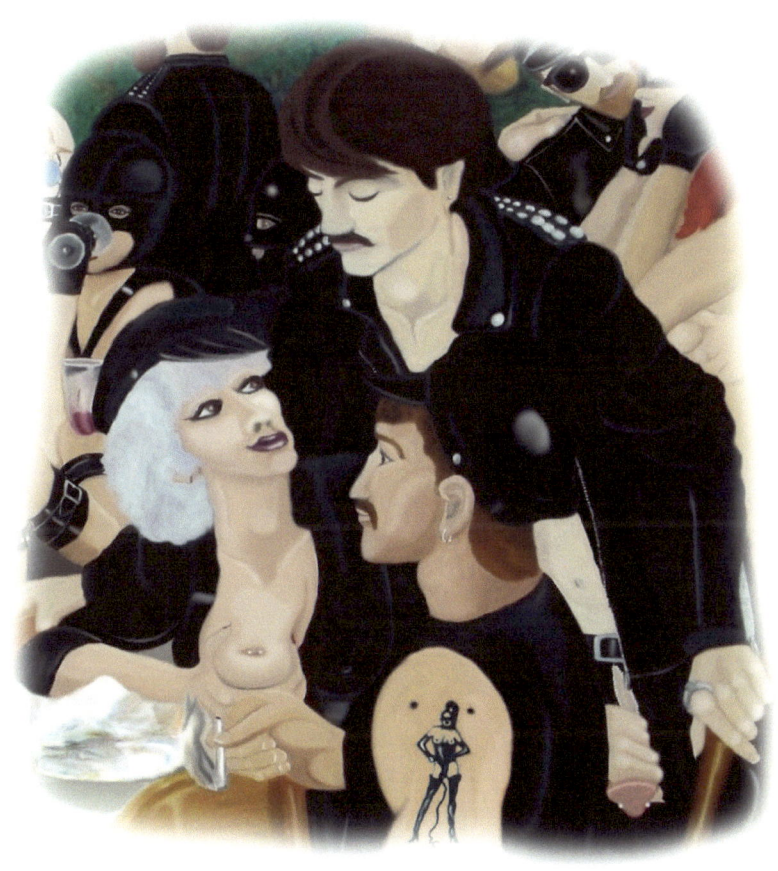

'If I show you mine, will
you show me yours?'

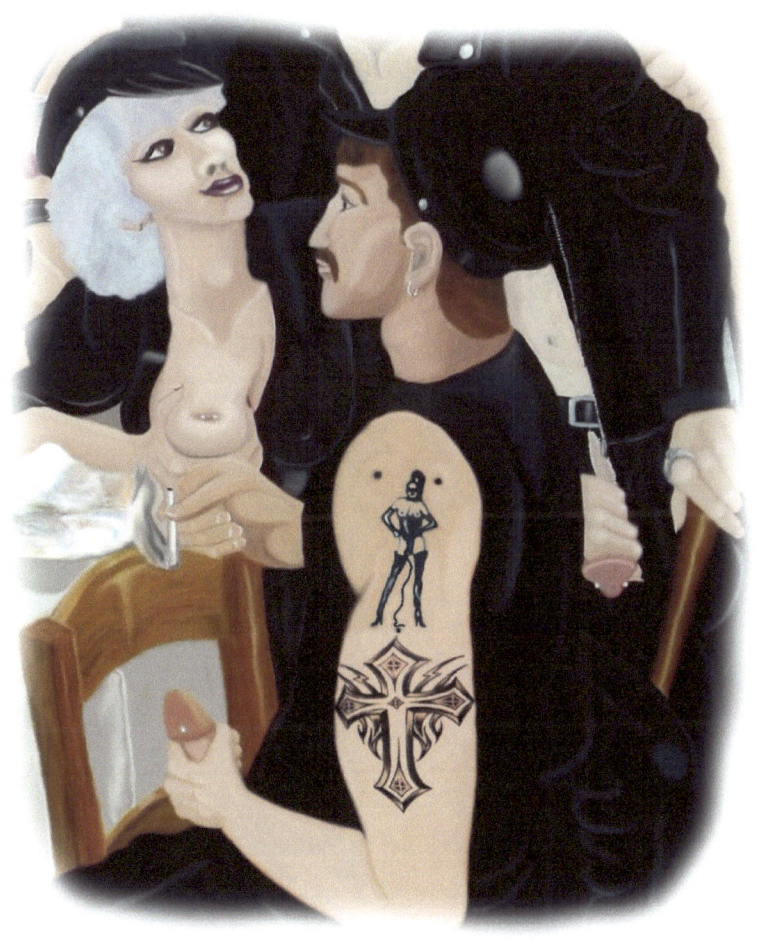

'You're not going to do
that in public, are you?'

'Also, take your will and fill of love as ye will, when, where, and with whom ye will! But always unto me.'

(AL, I.51)